# Watercolor Free & Easy

# WATERCOLOR
## Free & Easy

### ERIC WIEGARDT

Cheryl—
Best Wishes
1/31/15

Eric Wiegardt

AWS DF, NWS

Published by Harris & Friedrich
Little Falls, New York 13365
rfriedr1@twcny.rr.com

Edited by Rachel Wolf and Pamela Seyring
Designed by Brian Roeth
Cover design by Kayla Potoczny

Manufactured in China.
Library of Congress Number 2003114545
ISBN1-880166-03-8  (alk.paper)

## DEDICATION

*To Ann, whose calm assurance and unfailing support are a gift from God. To my children Nate, Zachary, Kelly and Esther, each a pocket of joy in my life.*

*To each of you, my love.*

## ACKNOWLEDGEMENTS

I start my introduction by speaking of the variety of influences that have contributed to my art. I wish at this point to acknowledge those people who have had such an influence on me. I have dedicated this book to my wife Ann, whose patience, support and love have made the context within which my art has grown.

Next to Ann, the most significant contributor to my art was Irv Shapiro, my mentor and friend. I cannot overstate what he has done for me. Most of all, he taught me how to think as an artist. I regret that he lived to see the book only in manuscript form. Bill Parks, another instructor, not only taught me to draw, but also wove important principles of life into his teaching.

My mother and father never stopped encouraging me, for which I am very grateful.

Velma Gorham, thank you for planting the seed, and thanks to Howard Cole for his generous assistance and photography. Dan Gerhartz, friend and artist, has over many years kept me on my toes.

My brothers and sisters, Mark, Teresa, Todd and Karen; thank you for many of the memories that form an essential part of the base from which I paint today.

Chuck and Gretchen Swartwout patiently proofread my manuscript. Thank you.

I want also to recognize the help of Rachel Wolf and Pam Seyring, my editors. Their gentle and understanding guidance have proved invaluable.

Finally, I want to thank Dick Friedrich for his invaluable assistance in taking my thoughts, both written and spoken, putting them into a clarified form, and using the scalpel when necessary.

All these and more have had a part in this book and I gratefully acknowledge their participation.

# Table of Contents

"Remembering Mom"
Eric Wiegardt AWS

# Introduction

I'm more interested in what something could be rather than what it is—I hope this book shows that art does not simply document reality, but that art takes us beyond the experience of our senses.

As I consider this book, what comes to mind immediately is the seemingly infinite variety of influences that have helped shape my art and ideas. In no way do I claim originality. We all borrow from one another; uniqueness comes with each person's blend of borrowings.

Tracking these various sources, I cannot but notice how very ordinary my early life was. Oh, I loved to draw, but so do most youngsters. Perhaps what set me apart somewhat was the intensity of my enjoyment. So many people think artistic talent is a gift of skill that one is born with; perhaps it is more a gift of passion.

The hours doing art projects in elementary school flew by! My parents encouraged this interest, taking me on Saturday mornings to Velma Gorham's studio, which, years before, had been a railroad passenger car. Remembering those mornings still brings a smile. And while I don't recall specific daydreams, I suppose those years must have included a child's fantasies of a life spent doing art.

Even then I wasn't much for detail—even as a boy, I painted with big, bold strokes. My style today reflects those early attempts.

During high school, my formal education went on hold due to other interests, but I continued to read about art and artists. Then I came to the realization that I needed to find my life's work. I took up engineering. It didn't particularly interest me, but I worked hard at it. While the days dragged, the years were starting to race. I had to develop my talents in some area I cared more about. Maybe I could make a living at art.

The next stop was the American Academy of Art in Chicago. The school showed me such beautiful work by Irv Shapiro and his students that I was more than ready to find watercolor as my medium.

To this day I remember doing my first watercolor. The elusiveness, unpredictability and fluidity of the medium, as well as the brilliance, transparency and freshness of the colors captivated me. But if I were to do watercolors for a living, I would have to approach this trade *as* a trade, not a hobby with the vague promise of making some money. I needed the skills, background and working time to develop myself. It was this decision that helped me get through the rigors of the program.

I realized, fairly early on, the futility of comparing myself to other artists. I follow my instincts. Of course, there are artists from whose work I learned and still learn, from Frank Webb, to John Singer Sargent. But there is no particular artist to whom I am beholden.

This book does not emphasize gimmicks or tricks of the trade. I include some techniques, but I've tried to be true to the approaches that inform my art, namely design.

This book is not an attempt to teach you to paint like me. By providing the approaches, the concepts and the underlying principles, I hope that you will be able to develop your own style, one that is direct and free.

Finally, I would say that it's hard not to idealize the profession of art. Though I have my struggles, slow days, unproductive times and failures, I also have the highs of new creative achievement. How it all works is a mystery to me at times, except the Lord has His hand in it.

Eric Wiegardt

# Some Information on Materials

## BRUSHES

Brushes, pencils, sketch pad, palette, easel and paper are basic tools. I believe in getting the very best. Yet "best" means what gets the job done to my highest expectation. Given that, you might think I have the finest brushes money can buy. But I'm hard on brushes, very hard. Wonderful paintings can be produced with inexpensive brushes. What's important is producing the best art possible.

I have very few brushes. My favorites are a 1½-inch flat ox hair, a 1-inch flat ox hair and a large round, size 16 (for some manufacturers it is a size 12). I also occasionally use a rigger for doing line work, and oil painting bristle brushes for lifting out pigment or for minor corrections and scrubbing.

I generally use the largest brush suitable for the job. I believe that small brushes lead to small thinking, a kind of tunnel vision. They tempt me to lose sight of the whole painting.

Get to know a couple of brushes well. Be versatile with them. Then, when a painting demands your full concentration, your attention won't be on a confusing array of brushes.

The size 16 round I use the most is a combination of natural hair and synthetic fiber. The synthetic is on the outside, surrounding the natural fiber core. This brush not only holds its shape well and has a nice spring, but the tip doesn't wear out as fast. In addition, it holds lots of pigment and water.

I see a brush not as a tool for filling in graphic sketches, but rather as an extension of the artist's mind and hand. I look at it as a beautiful drawing tool for self-expression, not merely a paint applicator.

## CHOOSING A BRUSH

My own criteria for choosing a brush are:
- It must be flexible, yet hold its shape, keeping a nice point.
- It must hold lots of pigment and water.

## PAPER

I feel more strongly about paper quality than about brushes. But my basic attitude is the same—I try to get the best that will serve my art. I use one hundred percent rag paper, acid free. Rag (cotton fiber) content and pH (acid/alkaline balance) are the two major factors that determine a paper's longevity. Acid-free paper has a relatively neutral pH, which means it resists yellowing over an extended period of time. Low-quality papers with a high acid content discolor rapidly.

The standard paper weights are 140 pound and 300 pound—this refers to the weight of 500 sheets, 22 × 30 inches. There are also different textures available: hot-pressed, a smooth paper; cold-pressed, a medium to rough texture; and rough. What you choose will depend on your painting needs.

*You cannot start where some other painter left off. You have to start where he started—at the beginning—and you have to start with the same integrity and the same interest.*

*—Kimon Nicolaïdes*

Hot-pressed

Cold-pressed

Rough

### Paper Texture

A factor in determining the character of your strokes is paper texture. There are a number of reputable manufacturers producing quality one hundred percent rag watercolor paper in hot-pressed, cold-pressed and rough. Experiment and find a texture that meets your painting needs. I do the majority of my work on cold-pressed surfaces.

## PAINT

Choose colors that are as permanent as possible. Check the manufacturer's permanence or light fastness ratings before buying paint.

Generous amounts of clean, fresh pigment make for strong color statements. Covering the palette with a lid at the end of each day preserves moistness. In the morning, test all of your pigments from the day before. If they can't be easily penetrated with a brush, squeeze more out. I always want to have more pigment than I need. It may be hard to accept, but most of the paint ends up down the drain. There is nothing quite so distracting—and sometimes damaging—than having to resqueeze more pigment when all my energy and attention should be focused on the painting. At the beginning of each week, I scrape the old paint off and squeeze on all new colors.

Watercolor, like all mediums, has its own characteristics. As you mature in painting, handling will become second nature, and you will develop your own set of techniques.

## FACTORS AFFECTING STROKES

A stroke of paint takes on varying characteristics depending on the amount of water in the brush, application speed, tilt of the brush and paper type.

### Wet Stroke
This is a stroke made with a brush holding its maximum water capacity.

### Dry Stroke
This is a stroke made by a brush with the water removed by pressing the brush firmly against a sponge or towel before or after dipping into the paint well.

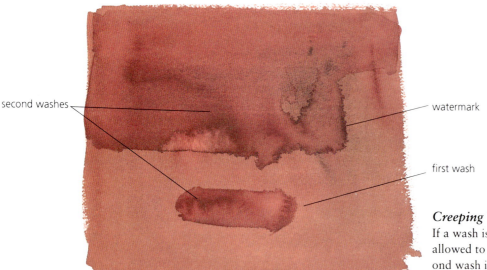

second washes

watermark

first wash

### Creeping Watermarks
If a wash is applied and the paper is not allowed to dry thoroughly before a second wash is applied, a creeping of pigment or a watermark will develop.

## MY PAINTING BOARD

My painting board is three pieces of foam board taped together with clear contact paper over the top to keep the water from penetrating. I began using it when conducting workshops, primarily because it's light; now I use it in the studio as well. I don't tape all four corners of the sheet to the board; I tape just the two top corners, thus allowing for the natural expansion of the paper when painting so it won't buckle.

*Broken Stroke*
I created this broken stroke by laying the brush almost flat with the paper and dragging it across quickly.

*Full Arm Swing*
I prefer to use the full swing of my arm—strokes are freer and less constricting that way.

## POINTS TO REMEMBER

1. Choose pigments that are permanent.
2. A good brush holds lots of liquid, keeps its shape, has spring and comes to a fine point.
3. Use one hundred percent rag paper.
4. Watercolor has many properties unique to the medium. Experiment with them.

## CHAPTER ONE

# ANYTHING IS PAINTABLE:
## Choosing Great Subject Matter

Honesty in subject matter boils down to being consistent with your personal vision. What it really means is trusting yourself.

There are forces that sometimes draw us in other directions. For example, it's both easy and tempting to check out current fads or scenes with an eye towards selling. I also remember thinking that using the same subject matter as better artists would improve my paintings.

One day, many years ago, I went to a nearby town with Richard Schmid, an artist whose work I admire tremendously. I naively thought that if I just could figure out what he saw, I could find the "right" subject matter. I watched him carefully (out of the corner of my eye) to see what scene he was shooting with his camera. Nonchalantly, I'd stroll to the magic spot he had stood on, then take the same picture. Unfortunately, the references didn't work because they meant nothing to me. It taught me a lesson: One's art should come from personal experience. You will make the journey unaccompanied, but it is richly rewarding.

# What Is Honest Subject Matter?

Honesty in subject matter requires choosing subjects that mean something to you. Relax and accept your own choices and interpretations. Be concerned about the viewer, of course, but first be true to yourself. Certain subjects, shapes and color combinations will appeal to you. So, like any other artist, you must follow the path of your current interests, emotions and passions.

Enjoy what you're doing. Take pleasure in the creative process at hand. That pleasure will show up in your work.

Trust yourself. You see in a way that only you can see.

**Fond Memories**
When I was a child, we traveled to Astoria by ferry, and the Gimre's Shoes sign was one of the first sights to greet us as we drove back onto shore. A golden goose in the store window held wonderful surprises for us; the memory still makes me tingle.

GIMRE'S SHOES

## DETERMINING YOUR PAINTING OBJECTIVES

I try to define my painting objectives early in the process by asking myself, "What interests me about this motif?" My painting objectives and interests arc almost always concentrated on communicating aspects of design.

What compels you about your subject? Shape? Color? Value? Texture? Repetition? Balance? The play of light on a vase of flowers? Try to be as concrete as you can. Perhaps you're drawn by the intensity of reds against greens. Or by the way light and shadow make patterns.

Once I know what I'm after, then I decide what will go into the work. Trees from one scene might well find their way into another setting altogether. Rivers, lakes and even oceans disappear once they enter my work—or are added to places they've never been in "real life." The important step is to decide exactly what I'm after, to settle on one point and go directly for it. If I have a house and a field that I like, I focus on one or the other. For example, I paint to emphasize the field (with or without the house). I can emphasize the house another day in another painting. Literal reality does not dictate; what goes into a work of art is the artist's responsibility—and its determination is based only on the artist's objectives.

*Favorite Subject*

In addition to being a favorite subject, a boat, with its many working components, is a challenge. I love to simplify those components while making them credible. I also love reflections; they give me the chance for expressive brushwork.

KNAPPTON TUGS II

## WHAT COMPELS YOU?

- Shape?
- Color?
- Value?
- Texture?
- Repetition?
- Balance?

# Gathering Reference Material

I always have my sketchbook and a no. 6B broad lead pencil with me. I carry my camera in the car. Be open to opportunities for data collection wherever you are; you don't want to miss anything. Be alive and alert to all the possibilities. Life translates into art.

I used to be intimidated by the sketchbook, thinking it should be filled with finished works of art—drawings like those by masters hanging in museums. Now I feel comfortable with smeared, smudgy, hurriedly drawn sketches. Field sketches or thumbnails are graphic notes that carry the concepts for finished work; they are distilled pieces of reality, one step removed from the world we see, one step closer to art.

## WORKING ON LOCATION

I am primarily a studio painter who works from reference material—photos, notes and sketches—but working on location helps me develop ideas while renewing my enthusiasm. Yet it is not always all that romantic; you might deal with mosquitoes, angry bulls, traffic, unfavorable light, inclement weather, wet feet and/or cold fingers. Don't be discouraged; know that location work will be the heart and soul of your painting.

*Finished Composition*
The essence of the sketch was relayed to the painting. Because most of the problem solving was done in the sketch, I felt free to express myself within the guidelines of the composition.

*Thumbnail Sketch*
I used to pass by this scene in downtown Chicago every day on my way to art school. This sketch is brief, but captures important, distilled information.

## HOW THUMBNAIL SKETCHES WORK

- Thumbnails are small, rough sketches.
- Thumbnails are noncommittal. You can quickly and easily do several for a subject with no obligation to go any further. You won't get that feeling of being shackled to a painting, because the investment is small.
- Thumbnails deal only with the elements you find compelling. They strip away distractions and give distilled information that can be used for solving larger design problems, such as placement and lighting.
- Thumbnails get creative juices flowing by taking one step away from reality, one step closer to art.

LUNCH HOUR

## WHAT TO TAKE WITH YOU

What you take on location depends on the weather, what you're going to do—and what you feel like carrying. Do you have a hike before you, or are you working from the back of the car? I always carry a camera with me and usually a sketchpad with a couple of pencils. If I'm likely to paint, I'll take a portable easel.

When I carry my paints with me, I also have quarter or half sheets to paint on. A full sheet is a bit difficult to manage. Once equipped, I am prepared for those moments when nature presents me with new subject matter, color harmonies, or any new combinations or ideas.

I see my camera the same way.

I do not take *photographs*, but gather *photo references*. The camera is a sketching tool. It helps capture structural, analytic data; it can capture ideas instantly, capture a moment quickly and easily. For example, such references provide information about how the boat is made, how the cabin fits, and what the sail shapes are.

## THE TOTAL EXPERIENCE

Paintings should communicate the artist's full emotional and sensual experience. Feel your subject, see it from all possible angles, touch it, smell it; in short, get to know it on such a visceral level that there is something in *you*, not just the *subject*, to communicate.

*Fresh Interpretation*
I decided to be very interpretive in color and shape here, yet still had the refreshing advantage of being on location. I left the white of the paper to represent my light pattern.

BENDICKSEN'S

## WHAT DO YOU WANT TO ACHIEVE?

Before going on location, think about it. Do you hope to:
• Capture color harmonies?
• Find design/shape relationships?
• Gather notes for later study?
• Capture atmosphere?
• Start a painting to be finished in the studio?

# Idea, Skill and Design

I am always reminding myself that the subject does not dictate; as artists, we may choose from reality what we want. We need not accept what we see. We can take reality and interpret it with our own design sense. Never be afraid to edit reality according to your own experience or what you want to communicate. Idea, skill and design make a painting, not a commitment to a particular procedure.

Camera, location, photo references, sketches, memory—I've seen good and bad paintings come from each and from combinations. The final judgment is the artwork itself. It is design that makes a painting.

## ANYTHING IS PAINTABLE

Any subject can receive new treatment, even if it's been done a million times. What keeps a subject fresh is an artist with open eyes. We have seen closeups of roses over and over, but we know it's a subject that can be done again, and done well.

I try to keep my eyes and mind open to the shapes, patterns and color harmonies in everyday things. A literal subject, landscape for example, becomes a vehicle for design elements that catch my eye and stir my emotions. For example, a snow-covered street is a white mass of a particular shape, set off by fascinating patterns. The pattern is what I'll paint, and the viewers' minds are free to see it as a snow-covered street.

*Be Prepared*
I was driving in the Willapa Hills when I saw this scene. Keep a camera handy when traveling, just in case you see an idea.

## DON'T JUMP TO CONCLUSIONS

Resist jumping to conclusions based on preconceptions. Learn to see the white mass and the color patterns, rather than snow and trees.

*Value Study*
When the ground is covered with snow, the world presents unique value patterns. The fence, tree trunk and dark patches of ice made an interesting pattern to play against the large, simplified tree mass above the figures. I added the figures for interest, as well as for scale.

*Spot Key Relationships*
With all the preparation done, this rapid execution is based on careful planning. The mass of snow reads correctly, because the value of the snow is right in relation to the other, darker shapes. Train yourself to see such relationships—if you get them right, the objects (in this case, the snow) will define themselves.

WILLAPA HILLS SNOW

## LEARNING TO SEE

Learn to trust your eyes; open them to the possibilities. Do not allow your mind to immediately tell you what you are seeing, because your mind will shape your vision, and you'll be seeing the same snow you've seen hundreds of times before. Practice coming to subjects without those preconceptions, and your mind will be free to understand familiar subject matter anew.

Many artists feel they have to travel to find "new" material and perhaps it does help. I think travel is fine, but not necessary. I do my best work with subjects that are close at hand. Objects I've seen all my life will sometimes surprise me. I'll see them as I've never seen them before.

*A man can only paint that which he knows even more than intimately, he has got to know it spiritually. And to do that he has got to live around it, in it and be a part of it.*

—N.C. Wyeth

# HONEST SUBJECT MATTER

### STEP ONE

*Laying Down Color*

Astoria, Oregon, is honest subject matter for me. Its sights, smells and sounds have become a part of me. They are essential elements to projecting an emotion, going beyond mere picture making.

This scene presented itself as a mosaic of strong, interesting shapes with wide value contrasts. I chose to use bold color statements. I began laying down rich shapes of color on white paper.

### STEP TWO

*Blocking in Shapes*

I keep blocking in my large shapes around the whites with fresh color. I am interested in the whites of the buildings as a value pattern. I do not hesitate to deviate, amplify or exaggerate the lights to strengthen my design, such as leaving the telephone poles the white of the paper.

### STEP THREE

*Finishing Shapes*

I finish out my shapes to the edge of the picture plane.

## STEP FOUR

### *Lifting as Technique*

I felt that the blue water was a little too intense. To soften it I dropped in some fresh water and lifted up some of the pigment. For the shadow on the road to the left of the yellow car, I used an oil painter's bristle brush to loosen the color, which I lifted by dabbing with a tissue. Additional washes were added later. Lifting as a technique is discussed in chapter six.

ALAMEDA AVE.-ASTORIA

# POINTS TO REMEMBER

1. Choose subjects that mean something to you.
2. Keep yourself open to new subject matter, even if it doesn't fit pre-conceived ideas.
3. Enjoyment in the creative process will transfer to your final painting.
4. Be specific about your painting objectives; vague objectives result in vague paintings.
5. Know your subject well. Try to look at it from different viewpoints.
6. Use a variety of working approaches—studio, location, sketches, thumbnails, memory and photo references.
7. Use thumbnail sketches to capture the essence of a scene and as preliminaries to studio sketches. They allow you to quickly try many approaches to composition, line or value masses.

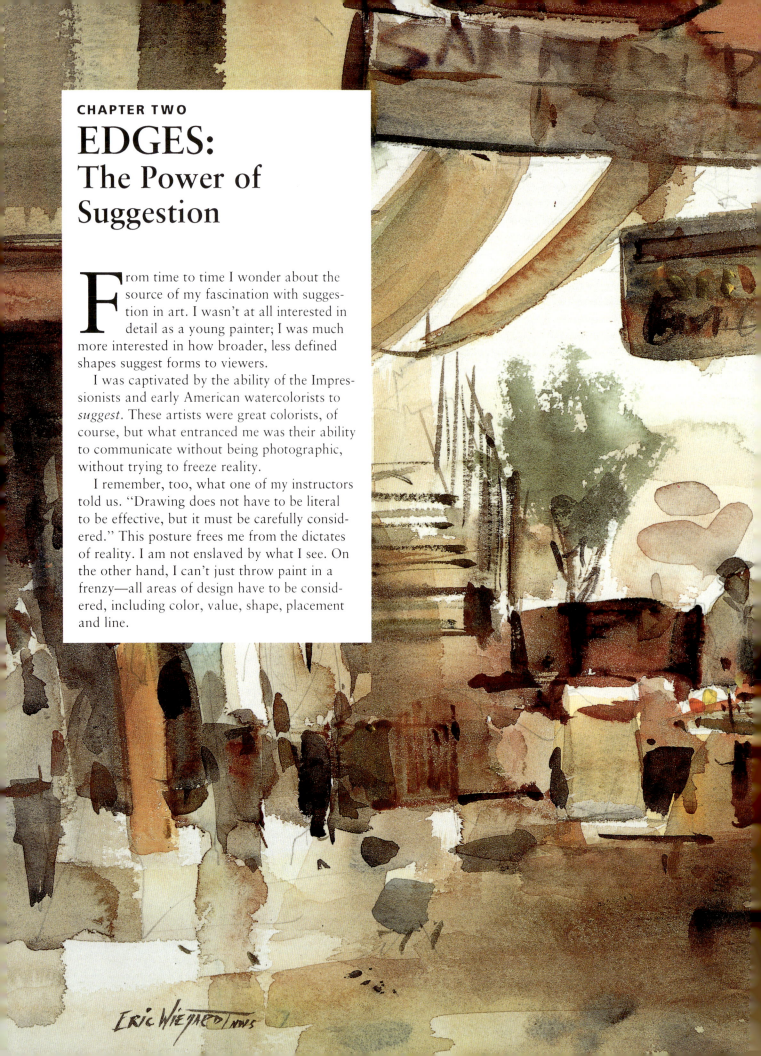

## CHAPTER TWO
# EDGES:
# The Power of Suggestion

From time to time I wonder about the source of my fascination with suggestion in art. I wasn't at all interested in detail as a young painter; I was much more interested in how broader, less defined shapes suggest forms to viewers.

I was captivated by the ability of the Impressionists and early American watercolorists to *suggest*. These artists were great colorists, of course, but what entranced me was their ability to communicate without being photographic, without trying to freeze reality.

I remember, too, what one of my instructors told us. "Drawing does not have to be literal to be effective, but it must be carefully considered." This posture frees me from the dictates of reality. I am not enslaved by what I see. On the other hand, I can't just throw paint in a frenzy—all areas of design have to be considered, including color, value, shape, placement and line.

Eric Wiegardt nws

# Working Between the Abstract and the Real

Because watercolor intrinsically lends itself to the brief statement, it is the ideal medium for exploring the power of suggestion. One conclusion I have drawn is that a slightly "false" but fresh statement is superior to an overworked, literally "true" statement. A stroke that is fresh and appealing, but deviates slightly from what we observe in reality, appeals to me infinitely more than a tiresomely "correct" one.

What I accomplish in my art depends on allowing the viewer to move from abstraction to reality. I provide the abstract; their minds provide the leap to reality. It is that leap, I believe, with the viewer an active participant in the work, that makes real art. Over-refining does too much for the viewer.

*Anyone can learn to paint and to analyze physical truths as facts, but few have the power of self-analysis.*
—John Carlson

**Every Stroke Matters**
The foreground bicycle is clearly defined, which in turn defines the other shapes as bicycles. The strokes are suggestive, but were carefully considered. Every stroke either adds to or takes away from your design.

BICYCLES AT BLACK LAKE

*Feel Free*

Feel free to be selective with what you put into a painting. I used only a few of the fence posts that I saw on the day I did this piece. Don't be a slave to reality.

FENCE LINE—OYSTERVILLE

## HOW MUCH REALITY?

How much reality should go into a painting? Am I trying to present reality? Yes. But the reality I present is inside me, rather than the subject. Each person's experience is different and your experience will change with new light, new moods, new you.

It is this shifting nature of experience that drives me as an artist. Knowing that no one has seen a particular field in quite the same way moves me to communicate my experience. I'm saying, "Here's the scene the way I encounter it." Art is what something *could be* rather than what it

*is*. I am more interested in a painting from the heart than visual truth.

I try to be honest with myself and the viewer, which means maintaining a high degree of integrity between what I produce and what is inside me. I interpret reality.

### Fresh, Suggestive Handling

Suggestion plays a big part in my handling of the lilies and leaves here. Every stroke is brief, direct and confidently placed. These fresh statements are superior to over-worked, tediously "truthful" ones.

EASTER LILIES

*Ability to copy lines, shapes, tones, amounts to little. Ability to correlate lines, shape tones, is the rare and necessary quality of the artist.*

*—Robert Henri*

### Concentrate on Communicating

Concentrate on communicating instead of getting things "just right." Realize that the sum of the parts, the design, is more important than any individual part.

DAISIES

*No great artist ever sees things as they really are. If he did, he would cease to be an artist.*
—Oscar Wilde

# Edges as Tools

In painting, it is traditional to discuss value, shape, size, line and color as tools. I also like to consider edges—where one shape meets another—as tools for the power of suggestion.

To give the illusion of a slow change in form, value or color, use a soft edge; for a rapid change in form, value or color, use a hard edge. Hard edges are more noticeable, drawing the eye to a particular area, while soft edges make the junction of shapes less prominent.

Look at shapes' boundaries, or edges, as opportunities for expression. Watercolor, with its spontaneity, lends itself especially well to beautiful edge quality. Be adventurous. Open yourself to the possibilities.

**Hard**
I applied the gray color after the red had dried, producing a hard, broken edge.

**Broken**
As this stroke progressed to the right, I allowed the brush to lay down horizontally, thus skipping on the "hills" of the paper, causing a broken edge.

**Soft**
With clear water laid down, I allowed two colors to mingle for a soft edge.

**Erased**
I used an eraser to remove the Cobalt Violet and create a soft edge.

**Scumbled**
Scumbling produces a variety of edges by pushing paint-filled bristles against dry paper.

**Varied**
Variation within strokes adds beauty and depth.

TODD & LEZLIE WIEGARDT
WEDDING FLOWERS
6/10/93

Eric Wiegardt nws
MOTHER'S DAY '93

### *Expressive Edges*

A variety of edges throughout a painting is a powerful, expressive tool. I usually try to run the gamut from razor sharp to lost and soft.

TODD AND LEZLIE'S
WEDDING FLOWERS

# Transitional Degrees of Wetness

An element of my approach that allows for exciting edge quality is what I call transitional degrees of paper wetness. Begin by laying down some washes on dry paper (areas should vary in dampness, so don't put an initial wash over the whole paper). Drop in other shapes and lines on top of those washes as the paper begins to dry. A stroke may go over a damp area, producing a soft edge, and end over a dry area, producing a hard edge. Make quick judgments, because decisions about each stroke demand an intuitive response rather than a calculating one. Besides, a stroke that loses its shape because it runs into an area that is too wet can be redefined at a later time when the paper is drier (the combination can be beautiful). This situation—in which surface areas are drying at different rates—is what I term transitional degrees of wetness. This process may seem out of control, but it produces an endless variety of beautiful edges.

wet paper, soft edge

damp paper, edge begins to harden

wetter paper, softer edge

wet paper, softer edge

drier paper, harder edge

damp paper, softer edge

all dry paper, all hard edges

dry paper, broken edge

damp paper, softer edge

all dry paper, all hard edges

Here I wet the paper with clear water and followed with strokes applied as the paper dried, starting with the top row on the left, and ending with the bottom row on the right. Notice the interesting variation of effects, especially the beauty of a stroke passing through both a damp area and a drier area. In your painting, I suggest laying down some initial washes, then working in additional strokes as the paper dries. The brush will pass through varying degrees of dampness, creating a variety of beautiful edges. These edges can be unpredictable, but work with them; they have a charm.

## DESIGN AND SPONTANEITY

Using transitional degrees of wetness is like jumping into cool water. Here it is. I'm going into it. Here I go. But don't simply plunge. Balance design and impulse. Produce a watercolor both poised and spontaneous, exhibiting freshness and structure.

# EDGE QUALITY

### STEP ONE

*Paint Through Similar Values*

I block in the flower mass with one wash on dry paper, allowing the shapes to blend, mixing in touches of Cobalt Blue and Cadmium Red for variety.

### STEP TWO

*Transitional Degrees of Dampness*

By holding up the paper and looking at it from an angle, I can see that the sheen is gone and the initial wash is in the damp stage. I begin dropping in the warm shadow masses of the azaleas, and some rich darks, allowing the variety of edge quality to be determined by the dampness of the paper. In areas where the paper is slightly drier, the edges are more crisp; they run together in the wettest parts. Because I work with my painting board at an angle, the upper portion of my initial wash dries first, creating harder edges sooner with successive washes.

### STEP THREE

#### More Edge Variation

To the right of the vase shape I ran a vertical wash of blue. Notice how the edge softens where the wash of the vase was still damp, and then hardens where it was dry. This kind of variation adds spontaneity to a painting. Allow it to happen. You can always come back later and redefine if necessary.

### STEP FOUR

#### Still More Variation

Starting to block in other objects, I allow the washes that come across the damp paper to mingle, while the edges are harder where the paper is dry. The loose effect is refreshing. Definition can come later. The bottoms of the cans were done when the paper was damp. Notice the mingling of color and soft edges.

## STEP FIVE

### Redefine Your Shapes

Overlapping strokes are used in the foreground.

BONNIE'S AZALEAS

# Using Lines and Edges

I remember a little girl who, looking at one of my paintings, called out, "Mommy, he doesn't stay in the lines." It is always tempting, when shapes and values are not quite coming together, to define these forms by drawing lines around them. But overuse of line to demarcate boundaries causes a painting to lose its sense of depth and appear flat. A lack of good edge quality makes a painting appear childish, amateurish. Lines function in a painting as design elements, so reserve them for this purpose. Use value to show separation between shapes, and lines for their design function. Beautiful line work is an art in itself. Notice the variety and change in these quick gestures of cows, goose and ballerina. Some lines are solid, others broken. Some statements (such as the ballerina's right hand) are left incomplete, yet sufficiently complete for the mind to recognize.

### No Lines Required

Form and depth are determined by changes in value and overlapping. Line work is not necessary to mark the boundaries.

### Unclear Value Pattern

The value pattern here is unclear. Line has been used to give form to the structures, resulting in a flat, amateurish look. Use line as a design tool, rather than a boundary marker.

### Value Defines Form

When value defines form, line is elevated to the level of design element.

# CALLIGRAPHY

## CALLIGRAPHY

The term calligraphy, as used here, refers to line work used in drawing or painting.

### STEP ONE

*Create Interesting Edges*

After loosely sketching the subject, I drop in some dark color for the window, letting it dry so there is no glare (the wash will be just damp). I then wash warm color over the face of the building, which creates a beautiful edge as it touches the damp window.

### STEP TWO

*Apply Lines Over Shapes*

I block in shapes as the paper dries to the transitional damp stage, then lay down some line work or calligraphy representing the ironwork of the fire escape. Note the variety of edges caused by the transitional damp paper.

### Continue the Thought

The upper window masses are blocked in, and I scumble additional washes in the lower part of the wall for texture. This scumbling texture was achieved with a relatively dry brush so the bristles would splay apart and the pigment would skip on the surface of the paper.

## STEP FOUR

### Apply Additional Calligraphy

I reserve most of my line work for the lower part of the painting, in the area of dominance. Here line work is an integral element of the design, not a boundary marker.

FIRE ESCAPES—ASTORIA

Hard edge

Calligraphy

Soft edge

Scrape done with the end of a brush handle

Broken stroke

# Wet Scraping

Drawing the chisel end of the brush (or any like tool) across pigment while it is wet leaves a dark line.

# Dry Scraping

If you wait until the pigment is a bit drier, scraping leaves lighter lines because it pushes the pigment aside.

*Scratching*
I use a razor blade to scratch dry pigment. This is good for accents and embellishments.

CRAB FLOATS

## POINTS TO REMEMBER

1. Consider the dimension that beautiful edge quality can add to your painting.
2. Experience dynamic edge quality by working with transitional degrees of wetness on your paper.
3. Use line as an element of design, not a boundary marker. Use value differentiation to show the separation between shapes.
4. A slightly "false" but fresh statement is superior to an overworked, literally "true" one.
5. Don't let reality spoil a good painting. Don't be tiresomely, mechanically truthful. Interpret reality by providing basic shapes and letting the viewer put them together.

## CHAPTER THREE

# RICH COLOR:
## Don't Be Afraid of Your Paints

Looking back on my years in art school, I find that things I have not thought about or used regularly have faded from memory, while other, more basic information still resides in the back of my mind. Color theory is a case in point. I gained a basic understanding of it through color wheels and charts, and as I have put more miles on my brush, that theory has simply become part of the way I work. What it boils down to are a few basics.

# Color Basics

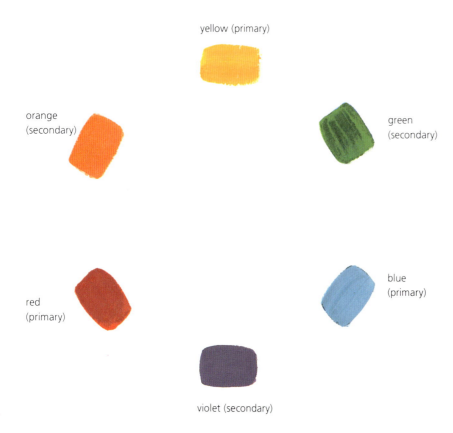

yellow (primary)

orange
(secondary)

green
(secondary)

red
(primary)

blue
(primary)

violet (secondary)

## COLOR WHEEL

A color wheel is used to describe color relationships. Red, yellow and blue are primary colors that can be combined to make the secondaries of orange, green and violet.

## PRIMARY COLORS

Cadmium Red, Cobalt Blue and Cadmium Yellow are primary colors that offer a wide range of color harmonies.

# Complementary Colors

Complementary colors are those roughly opposite each other on the color wheel. For example, blue and orange are traditional complements. But don't limit yourself. Variations of a color can also be used as complements, as shown here.

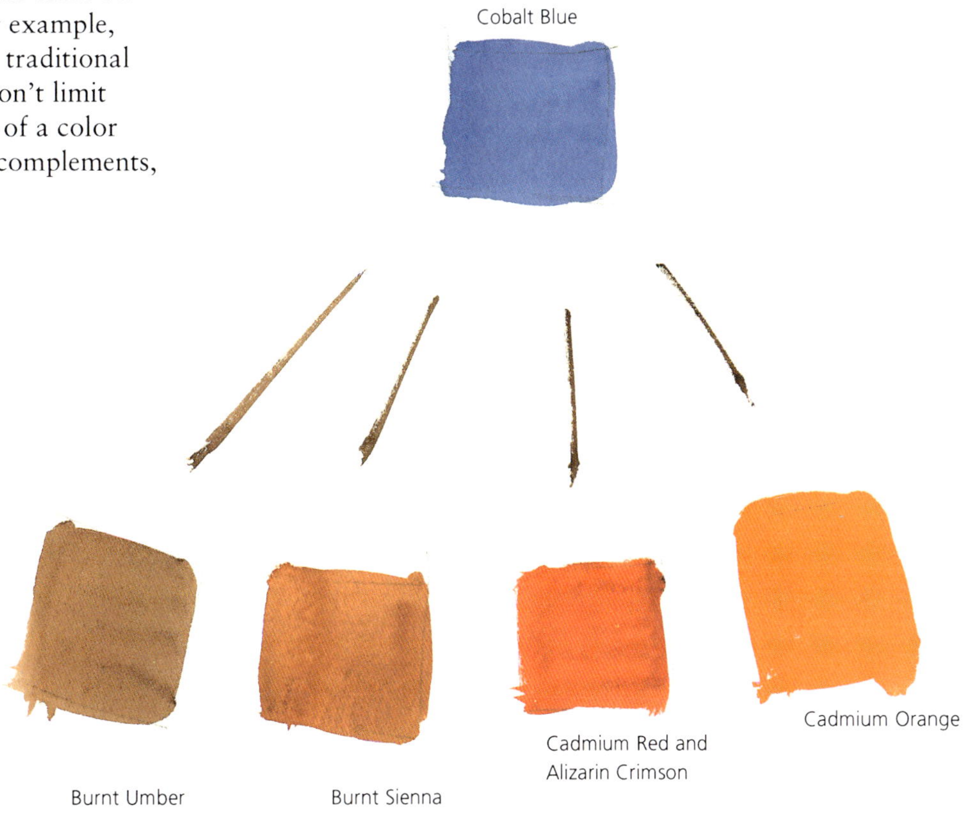

Cobalt Blue

Burnt Umber

Burnt Sienna

Cadmium Red and Alizarin Crimson

Cadmium Orange

## GRAYING WITH COMPLEMENTS

To gray a color, add its complement or near complement. This example shows how each complement or near complement applied over Cobalt Blue has unique graying characteristics.

Cobalt Blue

Cadmium Orange

Cadmium Red

Burnt Sienna

Raw Umber and Alizarin Crimson

Cobalt Violet, Raw Sienna and Cadmium Yellow

# Color Intensity

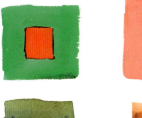

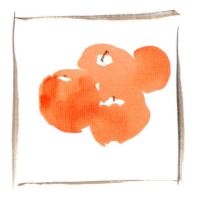

Equality of color is less interesting . . .          . . . than dominance resulting from inequality.

## ENHANCING INTENSITY

To make a color appear more intense, juxtapose its complement, or a grayed color. In the upper two squares seen here, the same Cadmium Red appears more intense on the left, when juxtaposed with its complement, Winsor Green, than on the right, with Alizarin Crimson. In the bottom two squares, the same Cadmium Red appears more intense on the left, when juxtaposed with a grayed green, than on the right, with a grayed red.

## VARYING INTENSITY

A problem can result from repeating color intensity with no variation, for example, the plate of red apples on the left. Let one area dominate with an intense hue and subordinate the others with a grayer shade (as with the plate of apples on the right).

## RECOGNIZING VALUES

Color intensity and temperature (warm or cool) are independent of value. The black-and-white photograph at right shows the value relationships of three graded colors to the left. Notice that red can be a dark value. Neglecting value means neglecting design, and, consequently, your painting. It is important to learn to recognize the values of your colors.

# Color Harmony

*Color of Light*
Yellow, the color of light in this scene, was first washed over the whole painting, affecting subsequent colors.

*Local Color*
Brown is the local color of the tree trunk.

*Reflected Color*
Blue from the sky is reflected in building and tree shadows.

*Intuition*
Trees don't have to be green. Experiment intuitively. The blues here aren't realistic, but they pull the painting together.

Color harmony is a pleasing combination of colors primarily dependent upon decisiveness (that is, not overworking and muddying your colors) and correct value statements. It is influenced by a variety of factors:

• **Color of Light**—Light bathes everything it hits with an influencing color. Thus, a warm-colored light makes objects look warmer, while a cool one does the opposite. A single initial wash over the entire painting surface can indicate the color of light.

• **Local Color**—This is an object's actual color apart from surrounding influences. For example, a red apple is red regardless of light quality.

• **Reflected Color**—Adjacent objects reflect their local color onto each other. For example, the red siding on a barn becomes greener as it nears the grass, which in turn picks up some of the red. To achieve harmony, I often extend this principle one step further, allowing reflected color between shapes that may realistically be quite distant but are next to each other on the picture plane.

• **Intuition**—This means working from a subjective, or personal, frame of reference. We can analyze what a color should be by carefully observing the color of light, local color and reflected color, but many times an inside voice screams out something different, and often better, than what is seen visually. By all means use the color from within.

# Color vs. Value

I have experimented with realistic to highly imaginative colors (even on the same subject) and have found the success of these paintings did not depend on color choices as much as design, specifically shape and value. Students often come to me concerned that they have great difficulties with color. In my experience, however, they don't have the problems with color that they think they have; if they're having trouble with anything, it is more likely to be with values. A former instructor once told me that color can be anything as long as it's reasonable, because values are what counts.

I try to be very conscientious with my value patterns. What that discipline does, then, is free me to use color as a way of letting go, of expressing myself. In fact, from time to time I use colors that don't appear in reality. Expressing color you feel from within can be a painting objective.

*With the general growth of a student's artistic state, this color sense improves and he will eventually* feel *color rather than see it.*

*—John Carlson*

### Monochromatic Value Study
Regardless of the colors chosen for a painting, the value structure is foremost. Working from this value study, the color possibilities are infinite.

Green and red juxtaposed make each other appear more intense, drawing the viewer's eye to an area of dominance.

Blue sky is reflected into the shadows. Cool colors dominate over warm colors in the entire painting.

This red is the same dark value as the green above it.

Grayed colors make the green and red on the boat appear more intense.

### Cool Colors Dominate
Using the value study, this painting is done with a dominance of cool colors.

ILWACO BOAT WORKS I

A gray color intensifies the eye-catching colors of the boat.

In the shadows I have pushed towards the violet side of my palette.

A gray-green shadow accentuates the warm colors.

***Warm Colors Dominate***
Here I have taken the same subject and used a dominance of warm colors.

ILWACO BOAT WORKS II

*Color may come purely from the imagination and, so long as the value and relationship is good, may be even more beautiful than in life. I do not consider that faking. That is understanding color.*
— Andrew Loomis

# Palette

Some artists work with many colors, others limit their palette. My palette is fairly standard. Number of colors isn't what makes a painting; it's how the artist understands the craft and how a design is handled. In fact, if someone told me I had to change my palette, I'd have little trouble.

My colors are arranged with earth colors on the left. As I move to upper left and top, they go through the color wheel: reds, violets, blues, greens, yellows. I turn the corner to colors I don't use often, the very intense colors.

## MY PALETTE

Burnt Umber
Raw Umber
Raw Sienna
Burnt Sienna
Cadmium Red Light
Permanent Rose
Alizarin Crimson
Cobalt Violet
Ultramarine Blue
Cobalt Blue
Cerulean Blue
Olive Green
Cadmium Yellow Light
Cadmium Orange
Phthalocyanine Green
Phthalocyanine Blue
Payne's Gray

## LIMITED PALETTE

One of my clearest memories of art school is that on the first Wednesday of each month we did one-color paintings. On the second Wednesday we did two-color paintings, and on the third we did three-color paintings. This has stayed with me because over the years I have used the lesson I learned from these sessions. It is a lesson that continues to teach me what is most basic to my artistic practice—that is, the *number* of colors one uses is not what matters. What you should pay attention to is value.

Many times I recommend that beginning students limit their palettes. I think of limiting the palette as a simplification that allows one's mind to focus on painting, instead of a bewildering array of color.

## FRESH-SQUEEZED COLOR

An important matter with color is to keep it fresh and moist. Even though I put the lid back on my palette at the end of each session to keep my colors fresh, once my brush doesn't penetrate the pigment easily, I squeeze out new. Rewetting the dry pigment might save a little money, but it only moistens the outer skin of the pigment, leaving the body stiff and unworkable. In addition, rewetting color means you'll interrupt the process of painting to work up hardened or stiffened color. It's a distraction, and it leads to uninteresting color and weak paintings.

## ANGLE OF THE PALETTE

Another consideration is the angle of the palette. I slant mine with a brush holder underneath. This way the water and pigment run down, keeping the working surface relatively clean instead of puddling in the middle. The clean surface makes it easier for me to work with more intense mixtures. My two containers of water sit next to the tilted palette, one for clean water and one for used.

## SIMPLE COLOR TRIADS

Limiting the palette doesn't mean just narrowing the color selection to the traditional primary colors of Cadmium Red, Cobalt Blue and Cadmium Yellow. Be inventive. Experiment with many combinations.

### Payne's Gray as Blue

This painting was executed with the triad of Alizarin Crimson, Cadmium Yellow and Payne's Gray. Since Payne's Gray is the closest to a blue in this triad, it takes on the visual characteristics of blue. Note the rich variety of color.

OYSTERVILLE CHURCH

Alizarin Crimson, Payne's Gray and Cadmium Yellow

### Burnt Umber as Red

This study of the Oysterville Church was done with the triad of Burnt Umber, Cerulean Blue and Cadmium Yellow Light. Burnt Umber is used here as the "red."

# *Adding Harmonies to Simple Color Triads*

Burnt Umber, Cerulean Blue, Cadmium
Yellow Light and Alizarin Crimson

### *One More Color*
Notice the additional color harmonies
created by adding just one more color
(Alizarin Crimson) to the triad on the
previous page.

# Broken Color

Watercolor is a great medium for exercising the power of suggestion. The mind seems to prefer seeing joined broken colors instead of just one flat color. Perhaps it's because synthesizing the colors requires an active viewer, one who is participating in the painting. Variety sustains interest. One color tends to lose its appeal, while broken colors hold the viewer's attention. Subtle color harmonies are just plain beautiful. Grays, for example, are ordinarily thought of as dull colors, but take on beautiful and exciting life when made with broken colors.

## OVERWORKING MEANS MUDDINESS

Muddiness is a matter of overworking with the brush—not of bad colors. What happens is that washes previously applied get overmixed into the current wash; the artist pounds the colors to death.

You can tell sometimes from the mixing tray whether a painting is going to have rich, broken colors. A rainbow on the palette promises excitement in the painting. Overmixed colors portend a muddy tone. Whether mixing on the palette or the paper, using only a few decisive strokes is best.

*Subtle Color Variations*
On the left is a flat, overmixed wash of Ultramarine Blue and Cadmium Yellow. On the right are the same colors correctly undermixed. Notice all the subtle color variations of the broken color.

*Broken Color Adds Life*
Overmixed and broken color applications of Ultramarine Blue, Cadmium Yellow and Alizarin Crimson. Broken color adds life to a painting.

GARDEN COSMOS

# Rich Darks

Many people who go out on a bright, sunny day to paint deep shadows choose colors that produce black shapes in a painting. In truth, however, colors exist in shadows. Perhaps we've been conditioned not to see them; perhaps the pupil closes down to protect itself from the light; perhaps it's simply because our photos don't show colors in deeper shadows. Nevertheless, the colors are there—step into the shadows and see.

In my art, I especially enjoy putting colors into the shadows, because shadows offer opportunities for a rich variety of darks. Be adventurous. Incorporate various combinations of reds or earth colors into the darks for warmth.

The main element in making darks richer is decisiveness. I do not overwork the colors but rather allow them to mix on the paper, or I strive to avoid overmixing on the palette. My advice: Get it down and leave it alone. I try not to use too many overlapping layers of washes for my darks, because that makes for dead, opaque color lacking the vibrancy of direct strokes.

## EVEN THE CAMERA CAN MISS

Even the camera often misses the visual information in the darker shadows. To compensate for this failing, I open the aperture more than usual to record that information.

### Gray, Lifeless Shadows
On a bright sunny day, if we were to gaze down this sidewalk, our pupils would close down to compensate for the bright light, and everything in shadow would appear gray and void of color, as in this painting.

One wash          Two washes    Three washes              Four washes

### Just a Few Washes
Get rich darks down in as few washes as possible. These examples were all done with Ultramarine Blue and Burnt Umber. The first dark on the left was done with one wash, the second with two, the third with three, and the fourth with four. With each wash applied, there is a loss of transparency and broken color.

*Rich, Colorful Shadows*
If we step inside the shadow, our pupils will dilate and see more opportunities for a bolder color statement. Knowing this, we can push color intensity, as in this painting. Compare the shadow areas here with those in the painting on the previous page.

## DECISIVE COLOR MIXING

Whether mixing on the palette, paper or both, I make my decisions and go with them. To achieve rich darks and broken color, don't overmix—a common trap for the hesitant, ambivalent artist.

# PRINCIPLES OF COLOR

## STEP ONE

*Establish Your Color Harmony*
I've decided on a conventional sky of Cobalt and Cerulean Blue. These colors are washed down to the ground plane, church and trees. This ties the ground to the sky, establishing a cool dominance. Warm tree colors, intuitively selected, are juxtaposed with the wet blue sky.

## STEP TWO

*Apply Rich Darks*
By establishing my dark values early on, the values of successive washes can be judged against them and the lights. The darks are applied with rich broken color from a fully charged brush. They are laid down with a minimum of strokes. Burnt Umber is applied wet into wet to gray the green tree mass on the far left, and to provide exciting color variation.

## STEP THREE

*Juxtapose Complements*
In order to draw the eye to the area of dominance (the church), I have juxtaposed the church's intense red trim against the grayed green of the trees. I then applied a grayed wash on the street, judging its value against the tree mass and sky. Note the varying subtle color harmonies within this gray—it was applied directly and decisively with minimal mixing.

## STEP FOUR

*Finishing Touches*

I establish more of the ground plane with colors reflected from the surroundings. The brown from the left tree trunk is dropped into the ground plane while the shadow across the road has some added blue to reflect and balance the color of the sky. I have grayed some of the intense reds on the far right with a wash of a complement—a grayed green. This puts dominance back on the church.

OYSTERVILLE

# Your Personal Color Sense

Decisiveness requires confidence and a faith in one's instincts. Early in my career I repeatedly asked what I considered to be a basic question: How do you know what colors to use? Slowly, after putting many miles on my brush, the answer came: There's no secret code, no set of rules. Painting, painting and more painting, along with careful observation, gives you your own color sense, and that becomes part of what identifies you as an artist. It's a part of your personal style.

I'm not convinced that the colors I see while on location are always better than the ones I sense inwardly. It's not just an easy way out to use the colors my gut chooses; in fact, sometimes it would be easier (and less risky!) to simply reproduce the colors I see in the subject. But "inner

Warm trees

Cool trees

Intense colors dominate in the point of interest.

Reflected violet

### Making Color Decisions

In order to bring out the color of the blue snow, I juxtaposed it to the warm sky. Notice that some of the violet is intuitively "bounced up" into the trees for balance. Although cool tones dominate, I dropped warm tones into the tree mass on the left for variation from the dark green masses.

SKIERS AT HURRICANE RIDGE

colors" often carry greater strength and more meaning than the colors that exist in the subject. Exploiting my intuition about colors, even at the expense of "reality," is not faking it or being unfaithful to my subject. In my judgment, I'm understanding color on a more significant level by expressing the truth from within.

When you draw on colors from within, you need to ask yourself some important questions:

• What color best expresses my mood, regardless of the object's "real" color?
• Do I want to convey a feeling of coolness, by letting blues dominate, or warmth, by letting reds dominate?
• Do I have strong shapes that call for a strong juxtaposition of complements?
• Does subtlety play a strong role? Should the majority of the colors be grayed with soft edges?
• In what areas do I want to intensify colors for dominance? What colors should be grayed for subordination?
• Shall I tone the whole paper with an influencing color or not? Shall I tone only part of the paper?
• What colors do I want reflected into each other?
• Do I need to bounce some colors simply for balance?

I take from both my own color sense and from nature. That's what art is for me—laws of reality originate outside the artist and laws of design sense emanate from within. Art draws on both sources, with some artists basing their work more on one than the other, but all of us draw from both.

***Colors Convey Emotion***
In this painting I chose warm, subtle colors to convey the love between my wife and our second son.

ANN AND ZACHARY

## Juxtaposition of Complements
The strong shapes in this piece call for a strong juxtaposition of complements.

### Subtle Colors and Edges

Subtlety plays a role in this piece. The colors are grayed and many of the edges are soft. This painting was toned with a cool wash over the whole paper before the shapes were given definition.

## POINTS TO REMEMBER

1. The basic principles of color theory are not complicated, and they are all that you need to produce beautiful paintings.
2. Color can be anything as long as it is reasonable, but you must carefully consider your values.
3. The mechanics of mixing a number of colors can be confusing. Start with limited palettes of one to four colors.
4. Don't be stingy—use plenty of freshly squeezed color.
5. Don't overmix colors on the palette or the paper. Muddiness is a matter of overmixing and overworking, not bad colors.
6. Limit the washes of your rich darks. Successive washes will lose the transparency and freshness of broken color.
7. Strive for broken color.
8. Remember that your own personal color sense will develop the more you paint.

## CHAPTER FOUR

# THE IMPORTANCE OF DESIGN:
## Big Shapes vs. Small Shapes

To me, design is the single most important element in a work of art. Subject matter, hard work, raw talent—all those elements play important parts; nevertheless, my art rests on design and the technical skills I have acquired to achieve it. The subject fascinates me, and from time to time I read—even study—articles and books on the subject. Nevertheless, I don't subscribe to any specific theory or procedure. I don't even think about the subject when I'm painting. To explain what design is, I like the simple definition in Webster, an "underlying scheme that governs functioning, developing or unfolding."

Though there are myriad elements to consider and a bewildering array of books, each one with its own approach, there still appears to be a common thread of opinion regarding what constitutes successful design. The heart of good design is simplicity.

### Looser Style

The lack of detail in this very quick and loosely suggestive painting does not mean that it lacks realism. Suggestion is a powerful tool and a bridge to the imagination.

OLD TOWN FRAMING

# Discovering Your Own Style

Style is just a matter of painting personality. My style is not something I set out to achieve, rather it has developed and evolved naturally. It is unique because it reflects my own unique personality. Part of the joy of being an artist is discovering your own style. It is not only a joy. It is the source of the art.

## LOOSE OR TIGHT

My style emphasizes looser constructions, but my perception and appreciation of subject matter dictates how loose or tight my work will be. Being committed to an unvarying style regardless of the subject matter or mood steals the chance to move with your art, to express the interaction between you and your subject. Sometimes I feel like working a bit tighter, sometimes I want the most direct statement possible.

*Tighter Style*
This is a painting I did when I was just out of art school. I love it because of the subject, but for me rendering of the face became a chore. Even though this subject matter and technique are popular, I grew weary of the need to be so exact.

ANN

# Volume vs. Design

Here's a problem. I often feel the obligation to provide volume for a shape. I like to think of it as the voice of reality. After I've followed the voice's advice, usually I wish I hadn't. Overrendering a form to show volume, to give it three dimensions, I lose the directness and simplicity of the shape—and, in fact, if I take it too far, I may lose the overall design of the painting. I would have been better off had I just left my values relatively flat.

To show volume realistically, you need to show many small value changes. But, with watercolors especially, too many strokes cause a painting to appear "muddy." Muddiness seems, at first glance, to be a problem of color. In reality, it is a problem of indecisive handling.

Simply stated, we have to decide: paint for reality (i.e., volume) or paint for design—even if it means flattening our shapes and simplifying our values. But the truth of the matter is that we can do both. There are times when there is strength in flatness and there are times when you need to show volume. But I always ask myself, if I show volume, will I sacrifice my design? Other times, I ask myself, do I need to show more volume so the painting will have more depth and a greater sense of reality?

Most of the time, I am trying to achieve both. It's a matter of craft—the skill and judgment that comes with experience.

**Subtle Value Changes**
This is an earlier painting in which I used many subtle value changes (look at the roses) to show volume. This painting turned out well, but I felt too much rendering was tedious.

LYNNETTE'S ROSES

Small gradations require many strokes that may lead to overworking an area, causing design problems and muddiness.

### Five Values

Rendering a sphere realistically requires many (actually infinite) subtle value changes as the form recedes from the light. Here I have represented five value changes.

### Two Values

Simplify your volumes into light and dark, represented here by two values. This example may look crude, but in the context of many shapes in a painting, this flatness helps to keep your design simple and strong. In addition, the colors will less likely be overworked and mud-died.

# If the Big Shapes Are Right . . .

When gathering ideas, I quite consciously watch for big shapes, because if the big shapes are right (in their placement, construction and assigned value) the small ones will take care of themselves. This principle comprises the basis of my design.

## THE IDEA EMERGES

I want pencil work to carry me to a certain point of momentum, and once I reach that point, I move immediately from the pencil to the brush. My objective is to paint; overpreparation wears me out. If I solidify the larger shapes by sketching, the smaller shapes usually present themselves in the process of painting. Sometimes, the beginning of a painting will show a mass of unrelated and unrecognizable strokes, but if I keep with the big shapes, my idea will come together, will emerge.

*Big Shapes*
I begin a painting by fully concentrating on the placement of big shapes and their construction. If you can capture the big shapes and values, then the subject matter will emerge on its own.

LILIES & DAISIES

# ... Small Shapes Take Care of Themselves

The larger shapes provide the underlying design of a painting, defining the smaller shapes in the mind of the viewer and producing the illusion of detail.

It's easy to see this phenomenon. Isolate details of my paintings from their structure by masking them off. What you will see are a few strokes that have no meaning at all. They are simply strokes. Then remove the mask and you will see that in the context of the whole, the shapes have become flower petals, people walking, awnings, streets, a grassy field or a tugboat's reflection in a harbor.

## SUGGESTIONS OF DETAIL

The small shapes stir the viewer's mind to see more than what is actually there. They are suggestions of detail. It is the mind of the viewer that provides them with life.

Reality resides, then, in the design of a painting. As an artist, I do not arrange people and trees, but their large characteristic shapes, allowing those structures, those patterns, to turn suggestions and strokes into people and trees in the viewers' minds. Designs communicate; viewers provide the details. I believe that this participation in the creative process is what satisfies the viewer. So, if the large shapes are properly handled, the small shapes really do take care of themselves in matters like drawing, color, value and edge quality.

*Small Shapes*
These small shapes are only strokes of color. But, because of their relation to the big shapes, the mind sees them as leaves and flower petals. The mind gives them definition. This understanding allows me the freedom to paint intuitively, with expression, when it comes to the small shapes.

LILIES & DAISIES (DETAIL)

## FREEDOM BY DESIGN

My work is loose, but I am really quite in control, because I am disciplined when dealing with the large shapes. Those large shapes, in turn, allow me unbelievable freedom to let go on the rest of the painting, allowing my intuition to take over, capitalizing even on the accidents of, for example, running colors. The latitude in watercolor is tremendous; large shapes forgive distortions in the details.

## YOU'RE IN CHARGE

This approach allows the freedom to choose procedures based on how you want to express yourself. Lay down a wash over the entire paper or just over a part of it. Start blocking in shapes without any underlying wash at all. Execute either foreground or background first, light colors or dark. If the large shapes are right, take any direction that moves you most directly towards your objective. You are in charge.

# Four Steps for Dealing With Big Shapes

**1. Thumbnail.**
Thumbnails are small drawings done on-site. They are quick graphic notes that carry the initial concepts for finished work.

**2. Studio sketch.**
This sketch, done in the studio and based on the thumbnail, is more thought out, though still loosely done. As you can see, I have altered values from my initial thumbnail. The studio sketch also serves as a value study, in which large masses are blocked in with solid values of lights, midtones and darks, using a broad lead soft graphite (6B). A good test for a strong value study is to place a piece of tracing paper over it to see if the shapes of lights, midtones and darks can be clearly outlined, as in the example at upper right.

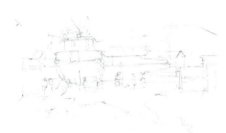

**3. Loose, light line drawing on final watercolor paper.**
Brief and simple, this drawing appears casual, but provides the structure for the large shapes. In fact, it becomes part of my painting. I erase only when it interferes with the rest of the design.

**4. Final painting.**
I am often asked by my students, "How do you know what colors to use?" My color thoughts gel during the development of my studio sketch; I start to feel and sense a basic color scheme. I go right into my final painting with no intermediate color study. Many times I have a general sense of the colors I want on a few shapes, and build the rest of the color harmonies intuitively as a supporting cast. If you feel shackled by the colors you see realistically, don't hesitate to exaggerate or manipulate.

DRY-DOCK AT PORT TOWNSEND

# SOLVING BIG SHAPES

## SOLVE THE EASIER PROBLEMS FIRST

A brief note about dealing with thorny problems that occur in any painting: I treat them just like the question of shapes. In other words, I try to solve the easier problems first, which seems to help solve the more difficult ones.

When confronting a problem, move to some other part of the painting where what you should do is clear. Sometimes problems can resolve themselves as you move through the painting. You may get rolling and re-confront the problem with more momentum and increased confidence. Sometimes, it's just putting a problem to the side temporarily that makes the solution come almost magically after a break from overconcentration.

### STEP ONE

*Initial Block In*

With a 1½-inch oxhair brush, I block in the large, obvious shapes—the pink cosmos flowers, the vase, and the shadows on the white cosmos. Connect shapes wherever possible and leave refinement for later. I'm conscientious about keeping my shapes simplified, with little variation in values.

### STEP TWO

*Keep Values Flat*

My concentration is still focused on chiseling out the large shapes. Once again, refinement can come later, if needed. Note the variety of color within the greens. Don't let preconceived thoughts about color close the door to more exciting possibilities.

The deep red cosmos towards the center is combined into the foliage, establishing a larger dark shape.

Small shapes are given definition by association with larger ones. Isolated, they are just strokes.

### STEP THREE

*Solve the Biggest Shapes*
Another big shape has been dealt with—the vase. Refined linework is added to the upper portion.

**STEP FOUR**

COSMOS

*Small Shapes Take Care of Themselves*
At completion, I realize excessive refinement in the white and red flowers isn't
necessary. I could easily have lost my light pattern. Resist the urge to refine
with detail prematurely.

# Painting Through Shapes

Now let's look at the problem of design in practical terms and suggest some solutions. As a medium, watercolor has unique characteristics. There is a certain unpredictability in how colors will bleed or how they will behave on the paper. What I call "painting through" the larger shapes—in other words, connecting them—allows the painter to capitalize on the uncertain behavior of the paint.

When two adjacent shapes are close in value, I connect them with the same wash. They can be delineated later.

## WHY CONNECT THEM?

The main advantage to painting through the large shapes is that I end up with a unified design. Connecting the shapes also relates them to their surrounding environment, just as they are in reality. For example, a red chair next to a gray wall picks up some of the gray reflections while the gray picks up some of the red. In fact, whether the color reflection from one object to another is really present, I will paint through the shapes to tie them together harmoniously.

## DON'T PAINT "HALOS"

I also want to avoid the look that occurs when shapes have a thin, white outline where the artist painted right up to their boundaries. These white shapes distract the eye, breaking down the unity and simplicity of the painting and creating "halos" around darker masses. They seem unrelated to one another and look pasted on. Their simplicity and strength are lost.

## EXPLORING YOUR OPTIONS

Painting through larger shapes gives the artist options in edge quality. As the shapes emerge, you can choose whether a particular shape will have a hard or a lost edge. Such lost edges give a painting depth, intrigue, interest. Setting hard edges early on makes them more difficult to soften later. On the other hand, starting with lost edges allows you to use artistic judgment later to decide if the painting requires more detailed information.

## VIEWER PARTICIPATION

Connecting the larger shapes also demands that viewers be more involved in "reading" the painting, which may extend their enjoyment of it. When the painting demands that viewers' participate, their eyes see only masses, and their minds provide the lines of delineation that exist in real life. Thus the painting becomes more "real" to them, while at the same time constantly shifting with their perceptions, remaining forever familiar and yet forever new.

LITTLE'S HOME, OYSTERVILLE

### Paint Through Your Shapes

If adjacent shapes are close in value, or if the shape you are painting next to is going to be darker, paint through them. In this illustration, other than the whites on the left side of the building, all the shapes are darker in value, such as the foliage. So I ran the midtone wash through what will later be darks.

### Add Darks

As I work in my darks, I can easily chisel out my midtone values without concerns about white "halos" around my shapes.

### Don't Create Halos

Here I did not carry my midtones through to what would later be my darks. When I came back in with the darks, white halos circled my shapes, making them stick out, looking unrelated and tattered. As small as they are, these white shapes distract, creating visual discomforts that have to be dealt with.

# DEFINING SHAPES

**STEP ONE**

*Value Study*

**STEP TWO**

*Wash in Midtones*

I first tone the whole paper with a broken, light-valued wash that includes some yellow. This underlying tone ties the whole painting together with harmonious color. Then I drop in midtones through all the areas that I know will be from midtone to dark. This creates a natural color harmony. The objects will then appear to be in the same environment of light.

## Apply Darks

While the paper is damp (the sheen is gone) from the midtone application, I start dropping in some of my darks, connecting the boat's hull to the darks in the reflection, thus eliminating any chance of a white line at the boat's waterline. Also notice that the background is kept simplified. By connecting the shapes, I have more control over my edges, and can choose later whether to leave them hidden (soft) or bring them out (harder).

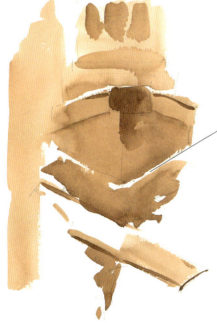

The hull and reflection are both darks—paint through them. Don't stop at the object's boundary, creating this white line, or "halo."

## STEP FOUR

### Define Your Shapes

As the paper dries, the edges of my strokes are harder, and I begin defining shapes
with richer darks. Because I have connected my shapes throughout the painting,
there are no white halos.

Harder edges and darks for delineation help direct the eye toward the area of dominance.

Strokes on damp paper, combined with darker strokes later, produce a painterly effect.

**STEP FIVE**

*Illusion of Reality*
Connecting shapes allows easy painting for basic design. Notice that, since the pilings and the hull were both done with the same wash, they have a similar color harmony. It does not take much detail to refine and give the illusion of reality. Also note that by connecting the larger masses early in the process, I have a variety of exciting edge qualities available.

BRIX TUGS, ASTORIA

# When the Big Shapes Are the White of the Paper

The principle of "painting through" large shapes includes connecting white masses. When the large shapes are the white of the paper, leave the connection unpainted, or paint with a relatively light color.

*Nicely Connected Whites*
Connecting your shapes goes for the white patterns as well. Find avenues to connect them into big shapes.

STUDIO DAISIES

*Poorly Combined Whites*
Here I thought "flowers," rather than overall design shapes. The whites are separated and disjointed, causing a fractured look. By separating the whites, I've caused them all to be the same size and created a static composition.

### A Strong Foundation
I've simplified and combined the light masses at every opportunity, leaving them the white of the paper. A strong foundation like this makes it easy to put in detail.

EAST POINT

### Poorly Combined Whites
Spotty and visually about the same size, these whites lack strength and appear fractured.

# Reserving Your Lights

I like to think of three basic values—lights, midtones and darks. Due to the nature of watercolor, the lights are easiest to lose. With each progressive layer, with each wash, the paper gets darker. Since the lights are so hard to retrieve, it's important to keep them available. I often delay working in those areas at all until near the end.

Too many paintings have lost their lights and their strength by too much guessing with the brush—you know, aimlessly applying paint with small strokes and hoping for a miracle. All it takes is a few strokes. So when I feel tempted, I put down the brush. Better to step back and think.

Remember—the white of your paper is not necessarily an unfinished part of the painting. In other words, it can be part of your palette. The lights are a critical element in a painting's design. Lose them, and you risk losing your design.

Of course, there are techniques like scrubbing and lifting that an artist can use, but I prefer to think of these techniques as more positive and active devices; I don't like to correct. I'd rather get it the way I want it by good basic design planning.

**Keep It Light**
Many times I will leave the decision to tone my lights until the end of the painting process. Here I left them the white of the paper. Notice the simplified figure on the left. Successive washes easily could have destroyed its brevity of statement, light value and overall shape.

THE BOARDWALK

## CONSIDER EVERY SHAPE

As a painting emerges from the larger shapes, it should develop a kind of balance to its design in its color, values and rhythm. This balance must be carefully maintained. Taking care of the larger shapes while allowing the little ones to develop does not necessarily mean ignoring the small shapes. In fact, as a painting develops, as it comes towards fulfillment, each stroke takes on increasing significance.

As a painting evolves, I find myself considering each stroke more and more carefully. Even the most casual stroke weighs in my judgment; often a single two-inch square near the end of the process will find me stopped, considering carefully before I paint.

## A DIFFERENT EYE

If a shape puzzles me, I move back a couple feet and hold my hand out to block it, looking at the whole painting without that shape. When I move my hand away, I get a better sense of whether that small part is contributing to or taking away from the overall composition.

Here is where I also find that mirrors are especially useful. Momentarily seeing the shapes differently compels me to evaluate whether the strokes and shapes belong as they are or need modification. So while a stroke may be a casual one, it cannot be casually dismissed.

*Develop a Balance*
As a painting emerges from the larger shapes, it should develop a kind of balance to its design.

SALMON CANS

*More important than the development of technique is the development of a good pattern.*
—Irving Shapiro

# Variety and Contrast

No matter how interesting the line, delicious the color, or well thought out the value, I find that going too far without a change destroys the very qualities I'm striving for. Instead of a passage that intrigues and satisfies, what develops is monotony. Dead value, dull line, dreary color—all can grow from going too far. Nature evidently requires variety and contrasts; certainly art does.

**Changes in Line**
In this detail, no line is carried too far without some change in its character.

## ENHANCING YOUR ART THROUGH CHANGE

Surprisingly, changes do not destroy the integrity of a passage; quite the contrary, they enhance it. Let's look at the matter of color. Putting in a bit of green enriches a red passage rather than taking away from it. Same thing with a line. A broken line is invigorating because it invites the viewer to complete the message, and I believe that engaging the viewer makes a painting more real, more meaningful. The viewer completes the picture by completing its communication.

### Changes in Color

Passages are enhanced when you allow changes, even if they're represented intuitively and not realistically. Look at the variety of color in these flowers, as well as the variation of line and value.

FIREWORKS

# Making Your Point With Dominance

Dominance refers to a picture having some point of emphasis, which represents an attempt to communicate an idea. Since I view my paintings as visual communication, I have to present a culmination of the various threads of the painting—in short, an area of dominance. Without this emphasis, a painting ends up being a confused statement of several ideas. While the center of interest is usually a definable shape, like a window or a single flower in a bouquet, it can also be a collection of shapes.

Let's look at some ways to show dominance.

### Center of Interest
Here we can clearly identify the center of interest, or area of dominance, as the relatively well-defined building cluster in the upper right corner.

OYSTERVILLE CANNERY

### Collective Area of Dominance
In this painting, the area of dominance is indeed a collective one, namely the group of figures, even though the figure in red is predominant.

PORTLAND UMBRELLAS

## VALUE

The stronger the value contrast, the more the eye is drawn to that area.

### Dramatic Shift

How have I used value contrasts to draw your eye toward the figure? I have reserved one of the most dramatic value shifts for the back of the shirt, which places it in high contrast to the background.

TIME OFF

### Value Contrasts

The eye is attracted to strong value contrasts. Look at the two squares in the centers of the dark ones. Our eye is attracted more to the one on the right simply because of the higher value contrast.

### Eye-Catching
The warm-colored red coat in a field of cool colors decisively draws the eye to the area of dominance, the figures on the beach.

ANN, KELLY, AND APRIL

## COLOR TEMPERATURE

Studies show that warmer colors attract the eye. Of course, warmth is relative, so a color can be a fairly cool one, but if the others surrounding it are more cool, the warmest one will draw attention. A classic example of this is the figure in a landscape with a red shirt. If all the other colors are cooler ones, like greens and blues, viewers will be drawn directly to that figure because, of course, red is warmer than green or blue.

### It's All Relative
Color temperature is relative. In both the upper and lower figures the center squares are a cool red, Alizarin Crimson. In the upper figure the square appears cool relative to the surrounding warm color; in the bottom it appears warmer in comparison to the surrounding color.

### In Context
Notice how red stands out in contrast to the surrounding complementary green. The lower figure has the same red square surrounded by a warm color, causing the red to stand out less.

*Cool Attraction*

Notice that one of the most intense colors in this piece is a cool one—the green trim on the boat. In the context of all the other grayed colors, it draws our eye.

KNAPPTON TUGS III

## COLOR INTENSITY

Independent of temperature, color intensity, or vividness, lures the eye. An intense cool color may dominate over a warmer color that has been grayed.

*Levels of Intensity*

Each of these colors is most intense on the left, where the eye is naturally drawn first, and becomes less so when grayed to the right with a complementary color.

## SHAPE SIZE

Larger shapes have a tendency to draw our attention—especially, of course, in a field of smaller shapes.

## PLACEMENT

As shapes are placed closer to the center, they become stronger visually.

### Size and Placement of Shapes

Here I allowed myself more freedom than I usually do in interpreting the shapes. The larger shapes in this piece draw our attention not only by their size, but also by their placement. A large white shape leads the eye through the center of the picture plane to emphasize the figures.

NORTHWEST SPRING

## LITTLE DETAILS

The more detail or refinement to an area, the more it draws our eye. I find this interesting, because details are just a series of smaller shapes, in a way contradicting the larger shape principle. And this too is relative. If a passage is delineated carefully, it will attract attention only to the extent that other passages are less detailed.

TIDEFLATS AT NAHCOTTA

### Subordinate Simplicity to Detail

I have reserved all detail for the oyster boats. Detail has little impact on dominance unless you plan large areas of subordinated simplicity.

## ANIMATION

Basically, I would say, our eye is attracted to anything that is alive. We find animate objects more interesting. Where this really comes into play is with the human figure. Perhaps we just like to see ourselves in the painting. A small figure will balance a larger tree mass. So the mind of the observer provides the emphasis, not just the artist's shapes.

## LINE

Line can be used to point or direct attention to the area of dominance. It can be implied or stated.

# POINTS TO REMEMBER

1. Deal with the problem at hand rather than molding it to a preconceived theory of composition.
2. Keep your design simple.
3. If the big shapes are right, the small ones will take care of themselves.
4. Assign a solid flat value to simplified shapes when sketching.
5. Block in larger shapes before tackling areas of doubt.
6. Connect shapes of similar value when painting.
7. Your lights are your ace.
8. Don't carry a passage too far without some change in line, value, color or texture.
9. A painting needs an area of dominance.

*Figures Attract*
As small as the figure shape is, we are attracted to it simply because it represents a human figure.

FIRST SNOW

*Implied Movement*
The movement here is implied by the broken line statement of the logs.

IN TOW

## CHAPTER FIVE

# PUTTING IT ALL TOGETHER:
## People and Places

Understanding a few basic principles of landscape theory will provide you with a framework for making judgments. Classically, watercolorists tend to paint from light to dark; in other words, the light values are painted first, then the darker ones. Such an approach is fine, but limiting. If trees are most clear in my mind, I start there and end up with the sky, almost a direct reversal of the traditional method. The fact of the matter is that I don't think that much about procedures, such as lights first then darks. I'm interested in what the painting is becoming; I let the procedure take care of itself.

# General Value Distribution

On location we see a logical and orderly distribution of values for the large masses of the landscape. The sun is the light source, thus the sky is usually our lightest value, even on a cloudy day.

The ground, when receiving light from directly overhead, as at high noon, is the second lightest value mass, while verticals such as trees or buildings are generally darker than their characteristic color. Birch trees, for example, even though white, are still darker in value at high noon than one might think because they are

vertical. It is important to remember that realistically those vertical white forms are midtones because they receive indirect light. Hills have a middle value at noon because they present a slanting plane.

This simple structure of basic value masses is what keeps your trees and houses vertical, your ground plane horizontal, hills in the distance, and the sky where it should be. Variations or modeling are usually needed, but not so much that it breaks up the separation of large value masses.

The preceding discussion assumes a more or less typical day when the sun is directly overhead. When the sun sits low in the sky, the light hits at a lower angle and values get turned around. A white building might reflect direct light and could actually be lighter than the sky. Exceptions might also include snow, or some other highly reflective surfaces, which amplify light in relation to the angle of the sun. It is important to understand these relative value masses so we can know how and where to manipulate them.

**Modeling Shows Form**
Values assigned to large masses need to keep their visual solidity, especially when you're modeling within those masses to show form.

EVERGREEN SUNRISE

### Values Can Change

When the sun is low in the sky and directly strikes vertical structures (such as a house), values can change from the conventional model. In such instances, vertical structures can be lighter in value than the sky, especially if it is cloudy. The white house is lighter in value than the sky due to direct light from a low sun.

CHINOOK

### Snow Reflects Light

Typically the ground plane is darker in value than the sky, but with highly reflective surfaces such as snow, this is often not the case.

OLYMPIC FARM

A vertical white surface receives less light when the sun is directly overhead, so it is a midtone value.

A horizontal white surface receives direct light when the sun is directly overhead, so it is a light value.

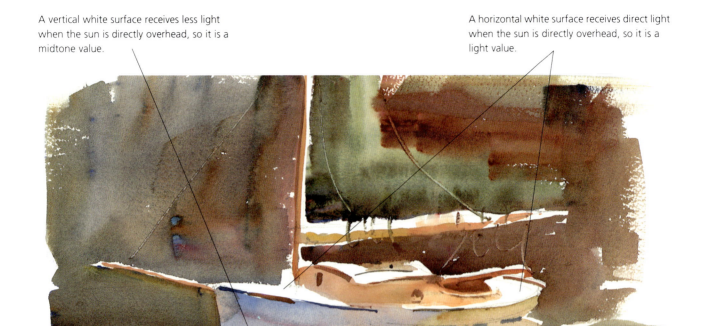

### Notice Values of Whites

Pay attention to the value of vertical planes that you think are white. Realistically, this is an all white boat. Verticals such as the hull, however, are receiving less light from overhead compared to the horizontal planes and are therefore darker than one would initially expect.

### Common Mistake

A common mistake is to see white objects and automatically assign them a light value, regardless of the amount of directional light they receive. This hull is too light in value, causing the boat to look flat, lack volume and pop out of the picture plane.

# Design and Purpose Come First

These general principles of value distribution are guides, not formulas. What really matters is to be purposeful, remembering that design is paramount—even at the expense of what we experience as "reality." When my design evolves and calls for a breach of basic value theory, then I break the rules. What counts is that deviations not look like mistakes. Be consistent in your interpretation throughout a painting.

**Design Comes First**
This light pattern, represented by the white of the paper, does not represent realistic values. Don't be afraid to manipulate and adjust your values to improve your design.

UP FOR REPAIR

# PAINTING A LANDSCAPE

### STEP ONE

*Sky Values*
With this painting, I wanted to capture the clouds that we see so often here in the Northwest when a sou'wester kicks up its heels. To keep the value relationships realistic, I kept some of the heavily clouded sky lighter than the ground plane. I also dropped some of the sky color into the foreground and water to establish a unified color harmony.

### STEP TWO

*Tree Masses*
I establish the tree masses, making them a much darker value than the sky. Assigning them a dark value defines them as trees. A wet brush softens the detailed edge of the tree line where it meets the sky.

## STEP THREE

### Foreground and Background

I establish the foreground mass. What is important is the overall value relationship. I pick out a few grass blades for detail and indicate or suggest the rest, being careful not to distract the eye from the area of dominance. I decide to make the background under the tree mass a lighter value for two reasons: 1) The strong value contrast against the trees helps draw the eye to an area of dominance; 2) The change in value from foreground (dark) to background (light) helps establish a sense of depth.

## STEP FOUR

SOU'WESTER AT LEADBETTER

### Figures and Highlights

As I finish up the painting, I suggest two small figures on the beach for a sense of scale and interest. I add a little more detail to the foreground, then use a razor blade to scratch some highlights into the water and grass. I make the grass mass under the figures warmer, drawing the eye toward the figures.

# Dealing With Foregrounds

Don't give foregrounds short shrift. Too many shapes in the foreground can threaten the solidity of the value assigned to the ground plane. Remember your area of dominance. If it isn't the foreground, back off on foreground detail. Many times all a foreground needs to recede is a change in value.

**Be Selective**

In real life, much more was happening in the foreground of this scene than I decided to show, but if I had gotten it all in, it would have distracted the viewer from the area of dominance.

BEARD'S HOLLOW

# Placing Figures in an Environment

We need not interpret the figure literally in order to be effective. Suggestion plays an important part here as it does with other elements of a painting.

## FIGURES ARE SHAPES TOO

What we have to remember is that the figure is another shape, an important one at that, in the design of the painting. Simultaneously painting the figure and surrounding space aids in keeping the figure in proper relation to its environment. I may sometimes delineate the edges of a figure to make it stand out, but I usually try to find a passage to let it bleed into its surroundings.

### Economy of Strokes
Suggesting the figure with an economy of strokes does not diminish its importance.

### Paint the Figure Into Its Environment
While painting the background washes I begin construction of my figures, allowing portions to bleed together, forming lost edges. In addition to creating a sense of motion and depth, the figures tie into their environment by allowing the viewer's mind to complete the lost edges.

### "Cut-and-Paste" Look
Here the approach to the background is the same except that it is painted around the figures, causing a cut out, pasted-on look from white "halos" and hard edges. Remember that the figure is another shape that must be integrated with the rest of the painting.

### Gestures Represent Figures
A simple gestural stroke or two may be all you need when placing a figure in a landscape. Broken lines representing legs suggest movement. As the figure walks directly towards the viewer, there tends to be a V shape from the waist down.

# PEOPLE AND THEIR SURROUNDINGS

### STEP ONE

*Value Study*

### STEP TWO

*Block in Figure Shapes*
The figures are gestured in, leaving refinement, if needed, until later.

### STEP THREE

*Construct Large Vertical Shapes*
Laying in surrounding washes, I tie figures into their environment so they won't look cut out and pasted on. Since vertical structures receive less light than the ground plane when the sun is directly overhead, I construct the trees and buildings of a darker value than the sidewalk.

## STEP FOUR

### Establish Darks

At this point in the painting I am usually anxious to have a dark shape established, like the one to the left of the figures. This gives me a goal post from which to measure other midtone and dark values. I block in the right side as well.

## STEP FIVE

### Block in Sky

I establish my sky with a light wash and leave some white shapes around the trees to balance the white in the foreground. I keep the sky lighter than my large vertical structures, the trees and buildings.

### STEP SIX

*Suggest Foreground Simply*
With my 1-inch flat brush I reflect the sky color across the foreground, breaking up the large white shape while establishing a color relationship between the sky and ground plane, keeping it light to preserve its overall mass value. For added interest, I suggest a bicycle leaning against the tree on the right.

MADISON PARK

*Suggestion of Figures*
An international kite festival occurs yearly on our local beach. In this painting I focused on the kite fliers rather than the kites. Notice the gesture and suggestion of the figures.

THE KITE FLYER

# Points to Remember

1. Understand large masses and their value relationships in the field. Don't hesitate to exaggerate these values to better your composition.
2. There is no right or wrong way to construct a painting. The best procedure is one that meets the artist's objectives.
3. As casual as the foreground in a painting may appear, it should still be backed up by careful thought.
4. A figure will add interest and scale to a painting, and need not be literal to be effective.
5. A painted figure is a collection of shapes interwoven into an environment of other shapes.

## CHAPTER SIX

# EXPECT THE UNEXPECTED:
## Learning From Your Mistakes

**W**orking in watercolor means working not only with the threat of failure, but also with approximation, uncertainty and excitement. Most oil painters make their plans, draft their pieces and mix their colors precisely. Watercolor, on the other hand, does not lend itself to such exactitude; it is a medium of approximation.

As a result, every painting has unexpected passages in color, value, shape and line. Even with a plan, a general scheme, you inevitably end up with surprises. But as long as the big shapes are right, these small, unexpected changes make for strength.

My suggestion is to go with these changes, adjust, be flexible. If you don't become horrified and desperately try to make corrections, chances are you won't lose the freshness, the directness and the excitement that are inherent in the medium itself. I only correct if my design goes awry. In fact, virtually all of the problems in my paintings result from violations of elementary design principles, not little things like drips and imprecise brush strokes.

# Fear of Failure

Failure is excruciating in painting, especially at the beginning of one's career. Over time, however, the agony diminishes, perhaps because failure occurs less frequently, or because we have learned to accept periods of missing the mark. Relax. More experience leads to less fear; less fear leads to less failure; less failure leads to more confidence; more confidence leads to directness and freedom.

## NO PAIN, NO GAIN

Of course, the threat of failure never disappears altogether, possibly because it's always ominous, scowling, troublesome. There will be moments when we can sit back and play it safe, or take the chance to go with an intuitive stroke, possibly causing a major shift in a painting's direction and running the risk of ruining it. What we have to remember is that taking these risks can make for great passages within a painting. We must trust intuition and allow ourselves to take such gambles.

### Accidents Build Character

In order to get the expressive brushwork and beautiful edge quality I enjoy so much, I did this piece rapidly on transitionally damp paper. With this approach, the unexpected is going to creep into my painting: Washes will bleed together, lines won't be architecturally straight, and sometimes an intuitive stroke falls short of what I expected. That's OK, and a part of watercolor painting. Remember to be flexible. Adjust to the unexpected and resist correcting. Keep your big shapes right and you will find that many unexpected accidents add character and flavor—in essence, your personality—to a painting.

BETWEEN SEASONS—ILWACO

## AN ATTITUDE OF CONFIDENCE

Having a positive attitude often translates into success on the paper. For example, when a painting is in process, a critical moment may occur when you're hanging between disaster and success. The fear is there—can you pull it off? When you reach that precarious point, you have to trust your intuition and act confidently. In the long run, it is better to be decisive, even at the risk of ruining your painting, than to be timid and end up with a weak, overworked statement. Painting with confidence is often the difference between mediocrity and excellence.

*The risks you are willing to take that might ruin, destroy or mess your painting will be the measure of whether or not any learning will take place. Worrying about what your finished painting will look like will inhibit you.*

—D.A. Leffel

*Confident Brushstrokes*
A positive attitude often results in success on the paper. My loose, fresh handling comes from confidence that I can draw with the brush.

# Decisiveness Wins

***First Take***

Working from a photograph and graphite value studies, I laid down an evenly graded wash of Raw Sienna, Cadmium Yellow and Cobalt Violet for this piece, followed by the boat and figure on damp paper. After letting the painting rest for several days, I decided that it needed additional texture on the left side.

Fear has no place in the process of making art. Timidity leads to dead painting; freshness and life come from putting anxiety aside, allowing you to paint freely and confidently.

One of my instructors had a good way to put it: "Don't let your painting know what you're thinking." Decisiveness will win the day. Make your strokes strong, free and direct.

## LEARN FROM MISTAKES

Work to overcome your fear of doing something wrong. Learn from mistakes and move on. It's part of the process.

*Success is not to be thought of as some shapeless goal; it should instead encompass the entire process of our development, discovery, and accompanying attitudes. In fact, what I think we ought to celebrate is our capacity to explore and discover.*

*—Irving Shapiro*

*After Decisively Adding Texture*
I rewet the paper, then let it dry to where further application would cause a desirable, yet unpredictable, creeping of pigment. I dropped in Cerulean Blue, allowing the process to begin, manipulating and tilting the board for guidance.

LARRY

## USING RUNS IN YOUR DESIGN

We've all been there. You've got this beautiful painting going when your colors start running. Before wiping up runs with a thirsty brush, realize that those runs may not be the problem you think. Let them go, and perhaps they'll become minimized as the painting develops. Or maybe this drip, this run can be capitalized on.

You can even plan for runs, anticipate them. If a puddle of paint accumulates at the bottom of a wash, just add a little water. Once the surface tension is overcome, it will run. Or just make the angle of your board steeper to initiate the run. Learn to see runs as potential parts of your design.

Look at watercolors up close to see elements like runs. You can see the artist at work.

*Great works of art should look as though they were made in joy. Real joy is a tremendous activity, dull drudgery is nothing to it.*
—Robert Henri

## RAINDROPS CAN BE GOOD

On location as a young artist, I dreaded the effects of the weather; too cold, too damp, too dark—always too something or other. Nature apparently refused to adjust to me. Since I couldn't really change that, I could either quit outdoor work or learn to gather information no matter the weather. I chose the latter.

Learn to deal with the forces of nature as a positive creative experience. You can either sketch and bring ideas back to the studio, having experienced the subject with more senses than just your eyes, or accept nature's contributions to your painting. For example, raindrops sometimes reach my painting and become part of the design.

*Raindrops as Design Elements*
I did this painting on location; halfway through, it started to drizzle. I decided to continue, letting the raindrops become part of the design.

THE HOPPER

## *Stay Focused*

Once you are focused on how to present the subject (values, colors, shape placement—your overall design), stick to it and don't allow changing conditions to lead you, unless you feel that the changes are improvements.

PORT OF NAHCOTTA

## *Graphite Notes*

Painting boats on location presents problems. They have a tendency to leave, so do quick graphite studies.

## FOCUS VS. CHANGE

In school, I remember the frustration of models going to take a break, then having trouble getting back in the same position. Now I work with the earth. Many things change, for example the

light—the model has moved!

Though models move, you are the artist. A color or value study may help focus you; as things change, that focus can remain, while still leaving you open to the possibility of improvements.

# LEAVING THE PENCIL LINES

I rarely erase my pencil lines unless they seem to intrude in the painting. I like the added dimension pencil lines give. Since they show the artist working, they become a special part of the work.

Like my brush strokes, my pencil lines are loose and free. I don't erase them when sketching. I leave them. If I need to, I correct right over them using the incorrect lines as guides. Someone once told me that if you erase a wrong line, you'll just make the same mistake again. For the most part, when lines just aren't working, I start over.

## LEAVE YOUR OPTIONS OPEN

Since I don't see pencil lines as boundaries but as guides, I leave myself open to draw with my brush. The more options you give yourself, the freer you are.

### STEP ONE

*Loosely Sketch in Your Masses*
Only occasionally lifting my pencil from the paper, I loosely construct a drawing of the masses before me, constantly gauging the relative size and distance of one shape to another. It is an approximation, a basic foundation. I also draw with the brush, allowing its interpretation to exceed the boundaries of the graphite lines.

### STEP TWO

*Continue Drawing With Your Brush*
After the red washes for the poppies are dry, I begin construction of the daisies by painting the shadow portion. Try not to see pencil lines as boundaries because that will create a paint-by-number look. It's hard to achieve fluid, broken color when you're overly conscientious about pencil boundaries.

### STEP THREE

#### Paint Around Whites

I paint the background with a 1½-inch flat, leaving the white of the paper for the light pattern on the daisies. The petals are constructed as I paint. The graphite lines serve me less and less as I base my painting decisions more on the emerging design.

### STEP FOUR

#### Refine Your Shapes

I have brushed smaller shapes in and around the daisies to establish an area of dominance.

POPPIES AND DAISIES

## DEMONSTRATION
# STAY FLEXIBLE

### STEP ONE

*Value Study*
Remember that a value study is not a blueprint. Be courageous enough to make adjustments while painting if the opportunity looks promising.

### FLEXIBILITY AND YOUR VALUE STUDY

Don't get locked into your value study. Sometimes painting value changes instinctively is considerably more satisfying than stopping your momentum to do another sketch. Be flexible.

### STEP TWO

*Use a Fully Charged Brush*
A 1½-inch flat is used to block in the yellow mass of sunflowers. If the painting board is at a slant, enough water and pigment should be applied so it beads up at the bottom of the wash. Keep in mind that runs tend to develop if you don't pick them up with a thirsty brush (that is, a brush that has been wet and then squeezed dry; if the brush is then touched into a wet area, it will pick up moisture).

### STEP THREE

#### Block in Large Shapes

A variety of darks represent the centers of the sunflowers. An unexpected run or drip happened in the bottom right-hand corner. I ran water over it and picked it up with a thirsty brush. A slight image remains.

### STEP FOUR

#### Vary Your Style

When a wash was laid down for the vase, pigment ran into the shape below. I should have left the drip I took out in step two—I put one back in.

This represents a different style from some of the other paintings in this book. Be willing to adjust your style to the needs of varied subject matter and your changing emotions.

SUNFLOWERS

# Washing Out Mistakes

If you really want to correct a passage that is simply not working, take fresh water and a natural sponge and try gently washing it out. Or submerge your paper in a tub of water for fifteen minutes, then just reach into the tub and gently wash away what you don't want. Believe it or not, you don't lose the whole painting. The rest will remain undisturbed.

**STEP ONE**

*Unwanted Passage*
Every once in a while I have a passage that I just don't like. In such instances I am willing to risk losing the freshness of the painting in order to correct.

**STEP TWO**

*Water and Sponge*
I like to use clean water with a natural sponge because of its flexibility and ease of use.

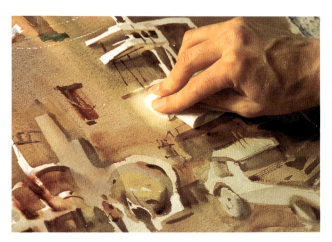

**STEP THREE**

*Picking Up Pigment*
Dab with a tissue to pick up pigment. Some papers release pigment more readily than others.

**STEP FOUR**

*Remaining Ghost Image*
Depending on the staining qualities of the paint and paper, varying degrees of pigment can be removed, though a ghost image usually remains.

## STEP ONE

### *A Painting That Went Too Far*

The right side has too many small shapes and looks fractured. It needs to be cleaned up and simplified.

## STEP TWO

### *Soak*

To remove a fairly large passage, submerge the painting for at least fifteen minutes.

## STEP THREE

### *Remove Offending Passage*

While the painting is still in the tub, gently wipe away the offending area with a natural sponge. A ghost image remains. Surprisingly, the undisturbed portion will remain intact.

## STEP FOUR

### *Painting Corrected*

I occasionally attempt a facelift like this.

# Lifting and Scrubbing

Sometimes an oil painter's bristle brush comes in handy. To lift a color, use clean water on the brush, gently scrub the offending part, and pat with a tissue. Be careful not to scrub the paint into the fibers of the paper. Let it dry before repeating. You can achieve the same results with a flat watercolor brush on a soft or smooth textured paper.

Keep in mind that lifting and scrubbing will usually not bring back the white of the paper, but will leave a ghost image. Many times a scrubbed-out portion of the painting will look precisely like that—scrubbed out.

**STEP ONE**

*Oil Bristle Brush*
To correct smaller areas I like to use an oil painter's bristle brush. For the smallest areas I use a no. 4. The bristles are trimmed back for more accuracy in lifting. With clean water on the brush, scrub the offending part.

**STEP TWO**

*Pat Loosened Color*
Use a tissue to pat loosened color.

**STEP THREE**

*Pigment Removed*

*Varying the Wash*
Variation within a wash can be achieved by first laying down the color, then lifting with a thirsty brush. The poppy above was achieved this way.

POPPIES AND DAISIES (DETAIL)

## REMEMBER THAT DESIGN MAKES A PAINTING

It is important to remember that design makes a painting, not gimmicks or techniques. For me, what makes a painting is working boldly on the large shapes, letting the smaller ones take care of themselves. Is it risky? Do I jeopardize what I'm working on?

In a word, yes. I read somewhere that every painting involves a risk, often more than one moment of risk. I am walking a fine line between something expressive and disaster. As my brushes get more miles on them, I meet those moments with an increasing degree of confidence. I know that those moments walking on the edge make my paintings more spirited, more alive, more satisfactory. That's the spirit of watercolor—direct and free!

### *Lifting as Technique*

My most successful attempts at scrubbing and lifting have been when I incorporate them as techniques and not as a correction device. To get soft lighting along the bottom of the center boat in this piece, I lifted out pigment with a natural sponge.

DRY DOCK

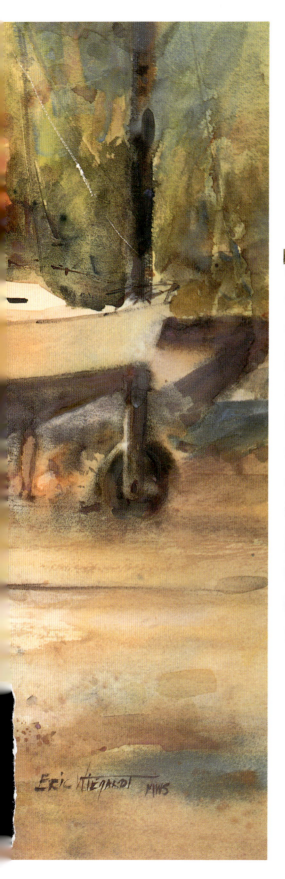

# POINTS TO REMEMBER

1. The risks that set you up for failure are also opportunities for growth.

2. When painting under changing conditions, it is helpful to stay focused on your chosen concept or design. You don't need to chase after all of the changing variables, but leave yourself open to new ideas that might be improvements.

3. Allow intuitive strokes or passages to happen. You'll make bolder, and perhaps greater, statements well worth the risk of ruining a few paintings.

4. Don't worry about unexpected surprises; most of the time they are incidentals that are minimized in the end.

5. Unexpected occurrences add character to a painting. They are a part of your personal signature.

6. Consider pencil lines a part of your painting.

7. You can incorporate drips or runs into your design. They have a casual beauty about them.

8. Don't be locked into your value study.

9. Lifting and scrubbing are not only ways to lift pigment for correction, but can also be considered a technique.

# Conclusion

As a beginning art student, I was somewhat overwhelmed—I had so much to learn. Skill, knowledge and efficiency come as you grow in art. Your judgment becomes quicker and more decisive. Your paintings reflect your experience.

Celebrate the successes, those passages in your paintings that surpass expectations. Also learn to accept the fact that there will be passages you might have done a better job with. Smile. Go on.

My art is based on design. If I have relayed some helpful principles and guided you in your painting journey, as well as imparted the thrill of watercolor, my efforts are amply rewarded.

Eric Wiegardt

DAFFODILS

# Index